COMBAT SPORTS

KARATE

Clive Gifford

FRANKLIN WATTS
LONDON • SYDNEY

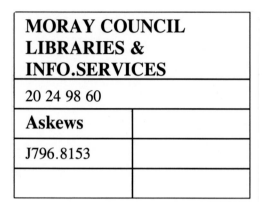
First published in 2008 by
Franklin Watts
338 Euston Road
London NW1 3BH

Franklin Watts Australia
Level 17/207 Kent Street
Sydney NSW 2000

Copyright © Franklin Watts 2008

Series editor: Adrian Cole
Art director: Jonathan Hair
Design: Big Blu
Cover design: Peter Scoulding
Picture research: Luped Picture Research

A CIP catalogue record for this book is available from the British Library.

ISBN: 978 0 7496 7875 3

Dewey Classification: 796.815'3

Acknowledgements:
Bandphoto / uppa.co.uk: 9; Columbia / The Kobal Collection: 4, 10; Jamie Squire / Getty Images: 5; Jed Jacobsohn /
Getty Images: 28; Kevin Winter / Getty Images: 11; Lech Muszyński / PAP / Corbis: 15; Lifestyle Photography: 8, 13, 16,
17, 18, 19, 20, 21, 26, 27, 28, 29; Michael S. Yamashita / Corbis: 12; Nadine Rupp / Bongarts / Getty Images: 14;
Paul Gilham / Getty Images: 24; Reuters / Kim Kyung-Hoon: 22; Reuters / Thaier al-Sudani: 23; Roslan Rahman / AFP /
Getty Images: 1, 25.
Every attempt has been made to clear copyright. Should there be any
inadvertent omission please apply to the publisher for rectification.

Printed in China

Franklin Watts is a division of Hachette Children's Books, an Hachette Livre UK company.
www.hachettelivre.co.uk

Please note: The Publishers strongly recommend seeking professional
advice and training before taking part in any contact sports. The Publishers
regret that they can accept no liability for any loss or injury sustained.

CONTENTS

WHAT IS KARATE?

What combat sport was originally practised in secret, and has been surrounded in mystery for centuries? Karate, of course!

Empty hand

The word 'karate' comes from the Japanese words *kara* and *te*, which together mean 'empty hand'. It is a martial art where people use parts of their body, not weapons, to perform movements for exercise, self-defence and sport.

Karateka

There are now more than 40 million karateka – people who practise karate – around the world. These range from schoolchildren to superstars, including glamorous actresses such as Lucy Liu and Jenny McCarthy and Hollywood big-hitters such as Chuck Norris and Jackie Chan.

Lucy Liu (far left) stars as Alex Munday in Charlie's Angels, *alongside Cameron Diaz and Drew Barrymore.*

Respect for all styles
There are many different styles or schools of karate, including Shotokan and Goju-ryu karate. All teach karateka to respect other styles as well as respecting their teachers and classmates.

KARATE BENEFITS
Students enjoy karate because it:
* is a great way to get fit and build strength
* builds confidence
* teaches respect and discipline
* in real danger, it can be used for self-defence
* is fun and challenging to learn.

A ROYAL SPORT
The Crown Prince of the United Arab Emirates and ruler of Dubai, Sheik Mohammad Bin Rashid Al Maktoum is a karateka. In 2006, his daughter, Maitha (above, left), became the first Arab woman to win a medal in karate at the Asian Games.

KARATE'S ORIGINS

Unlike many combat sports, karate began in one region: Okinawa and the other Ryukyu islands off the south coast of Japan.

No weapons

In 1477, King Sho Shin banned his people – the islanders of Okinawa – from carrying weapons. This ban continued after the islands were invaded by the Japanese in 1609.

To defend themselves, the islanders practised forms of unarmed combat, some of which came from Ancient China. Over centuries of practising in secret, these developed into what we know as karate.

Gichin Funakoshi (fourth from left) poses with other karate masters in the 1930s.

Shoto's karate

Gichin Funakoshi (1868–1957) was a schoolteacher and poet who wrote under the name Shoto. He had first learned karate in secret on Okinawa during the ban. In 1902, karate was taught in schools for the first time. Funakoshi taught students and became the founder of the Shotokan school of karate.

Big in Japan

Gichin Funakoshi took karate from Okinawa to mainland Japan in 1916. He displayed his skills in demonstrations and impressed many people, including the man who would later become Emperor Hirohito of Japan. Slowly, karate spread through Japan.

Karate demonstrations, such as this one at Shuri Castle, Okinawa, took place throughout Japan in the early twentieth century.

"The ultimate aim of karate lies not in victory or defeat, but in the perfection of the character of its participants."
– *Gichin Funakoshi.*

KARATE SPREADS AROUND THE WORLD

From Japan, Japanese masters and their students travelled all over the world, taking their skills with them.

Teaching abroad

From the 1950s onwards, Gichin Funakoshi's top students began to move abroad to teach karate in the USA and Europe. Keinosuke 'Tiger' Enoeda (1935–2003), for example, went to Liverpool, England in 1965 and formed the Karate Union of Great Britain. He remained in the UK for the rest of his life.

American karate

After World War II (1939–45), US soldiers occupied parts of Japan including Okinawa. There, they learned about karate and took their knowledge home with them. Hundreds of karate schools began to open in the USA.

Keinosuke Enoeda, a 9th-dan black belt, took Shotokan karate to England.

Karate Elvis

The 'King' of rock 'n' roll, Elvis Presley (1935–77) first trained in karate when in the US Army in 1959. By 1970, he had risen to an 8th-dan black belt (see page 13) – a very high level of karate.

Elvis Presley also starred in movies where he displayed his karate skills – bringing karate to a wider audience.

SCHOOLS OF KARATE

There are four main schools or styles of karate:
* Shotokan – Gichin Funakoshi's school of karate, the most common form of karate today.
* Goju-ryu – this school has more emphasis on strength training than Shotokan.
* Shito-ryu – founded in 1928 by Kenwa Mabuni (1889–1952), this features short, fast movements.
* Wado-ryu – created in the early 1930s, this involves holds and some moves taken from another Japanese martial art, ju-jitsu.

"As a student of the martial arts, Elvis was one of the best. He was physically strong and his technique was excellent."
– *Kang Rhee, Elvis's karate instructor.*

KARATE AT THE MOVIES

With its fast moves, it is no surprise that karate has featured in many movies. These range from explosive Asian martial arts films to family-friendly flicks such as *The Karate Kid* series.

He taught him the secret to Karate lies in the mind and heart. Not in the hands.

The Karate Kid

COLUMBIA PICTURES Presents
A JERRY WEINTRAUB Production of A JOHN G. AVILDSEN Film
"THE KARATE KID"
Starring RALPH MACCHIO · NORIYUKI "PAT" MORITA · ELISABETH SHUE
Music by BILL CONTI   Music Supervisor BROOKS ARTHUR
Executive Producer R.J. LOUIS   Written by ROBERT MARK KAMEN
Produced by JERRY WEINTRAUB   Directed by JOHN G. AVILDSEN

In The Karate Kid *a young boy learns the ways of karate from an old master called Mr Miyagi. The film was a huge hit and inspired thousands of people to join karate schools.*

Hong Kong action

Many action films featuring karate and other martial arts were produced in Japan, China, and especially Hong Kong, in the 1960s and 1970s. Bruce Lee was the biggest star but others, such as karate champions Sonny Chiba and Jackie Chan, went on to make big-budget, blockbuster movies. Many people in Europe and the USA saw the movies and took up karate as a result.

Students turned stars

Former students of karate went on to become major action and martial arts movie stars themselves. These include Chuck Norris and Dolph Lundgren who won European championships in karate in 1980 and 1981.

Super Sonny Chiba

Sonny Chiba played karate pioneer Masutatsu Oyama in three films, *Champion of Death* (1975), *Karate Bearfighter* (1975), and *Karate for Life* (1977).

Sonny Chiba, seen here with Lucy Liu, at the premier of a film in which he played master sword maker Hattori Hanzo.

AT THE DOJO

Dojo means a sacred space used for karate or other martial arts. Students entering a *dojo* are expected to behave according to the five *dojo kun,* or 'rules'. Students also wear a special uniform.

These karate students are practising in a dojo.

Karate gi

A *gi* is a karate uniform. The jacket and trousers are made of strong, hard-wearing cotton. The sleeves and legs of a *gi* are loose to allow lots of freedom of movement. A *gi* must respected; it is washed and folded when not in use.

THE FIVE DOJO KUN

* Seek perfection of character
* Be faithful
* Endeavour and persevere
* Respect others
* Refrain from violent behaviour

Belting up

A karate jacket is tied using a large belt, or *obi*. Different coloured *obi* show the level the student has achieved. The colour order varies for different schools of karate, but usually beginners start with a white belt and progress up through the colours, often orange, yellow, green, brown and, finally, black. Black belt kareteka can continue to progress. They start at 1st dan. The highest level of all is 10th dan.

TIE N' DYE

Gichin Funakoshi borrowed judo's coloured belt system in the 1920s and applied it to karate. At first, the white belt that kareteka wore was simply dyed a new colour – the reason why the colour belts went from light to dark!

A junior karate student has progressed to the next level and is presented with a new obi.

KARATE TODAY

Karate features three major activities. *Kumite* is sparring techniques (see pages 22–23). *Kata* and *kihon* are the other two main activities.

Kata

A *kata* is a pattern of moves performed in a row. It can look like a beautiful but deadly dance. *Kata* feature many of the important kicks, punches and blocks learned in training, mixed with steps and turns. There are over 100 different types and styles.

Students perform a kata *featuring a low cross block.*

Kihon

Kihon means basic principles and includes learning the movements and positions required for the main strikes, punches, blocks and kicks. Learning about stances (*dachi*) is an important part of *kihon*. All moves begin from the correct stance as this provides a solid base for balancing.

TAMASHIWARA

The word *tamashiwara* means strength testing by breaking various objects, from ice to concrete. It is rarely a part of karate instruction but is popular on TV and in demonstrations. In September 2007, Ali Bahçetepe from Turkey broke 317 concrete blocks in one minute.

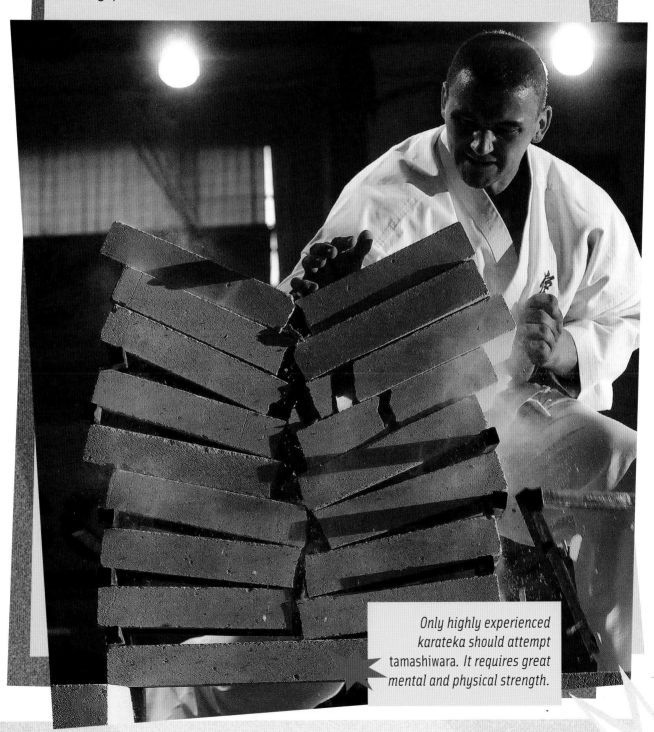

Only highly experienced karateka should attempt tamashiwara. It requires great mental and physical strength.

TOP 10 KARATE MOVES 1–3

There are lots of moves in karate but most start from one of the small number of stances. The three moves shown here can all begin from a front stance known as *zenkutsu dachi*.

1 Mae geri (front kick)

Mae geri, or front kick, is a fast kick that is difficult to defend against. The karateka raises his knee to waist height then snaps his lower leg forward, with the foot pointing forward but the toes pulled back. The striking area is the ball of the foot. The hips are thrust forward to add speed to the kick with the other leg bent to help balance.

2 Oi-zuki (lunge punch)

Oi-zuki is one of the first moves karateka learn. The front fist is pulled back to generate power as the other fist thrusts forwards with a straight arm. At the same time, the attacking karateka steps forward into the move.

3 Yoko geri (side kick)

It takes excellent balance and quick, fluid movements to perform a good side kick, or *yoko geri*. The karateka brings her knee up high, twists sideways and then thrusts her leg forward from the side. The striking area is the heel or the side of the foot.

MIND AND BODY

Karate is about improving the mind and body and getting them to work together.

Pause and focus

Before beginning a karate class, students spend a few minutes calming and clearing their mind of thoughts other than karate. This is called meditating and is performed in a kneeling position, sometimes with the head lowered.

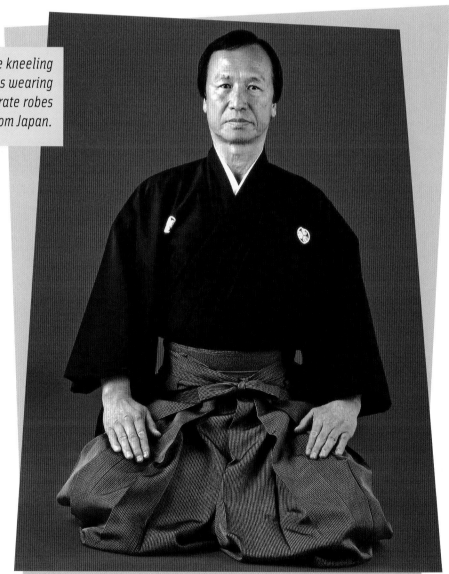

This karateka is in the kneeling position. He is wearing traditional karate robes from Japan.

The three 'R's

Respect for others and oneself is a vital part of the philosophy behind karate. There are two other important 'R' words – routine and responsibility. Routine is something performed regularly. Karate practice and attitudes should become part of daily life.

Responsibility

Responsibility in karate means being in control of your words and actions in the *dojo* and elsewhere. Responsible karateka control their movements so that they do not touch or strike a fellow student during training. They also do not use their karate skills outside the *dojo* to hurt or threaten.

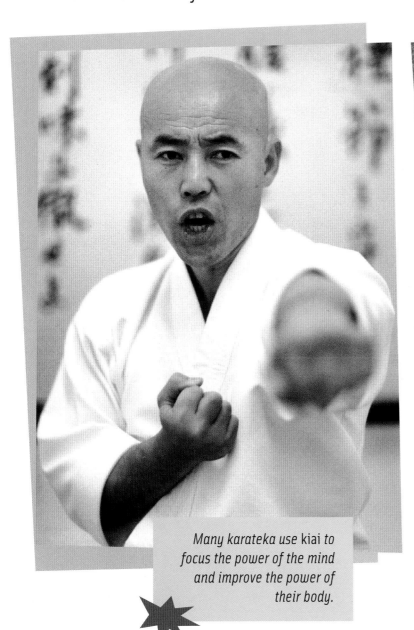

Many karateka use kiai *to focus the power of the mind and improve the power of their body.*

"Karate may be referred to as the conflict within yourself, or a life-long marathon which can be won only through self-discipline, hard training, and your own creative efforts."
– *Shoshin Nagamine (1907–97), legendary Okinawa karate instructor.*

Power of kiai

Skilled karateka can summon extra strength during training using a shout called *kiai*. *Kiai* is more than just a battle-cry, it is the release of focused energy from inside the body. Some karateka also use *kiai* to prepare themselves for difficult tasks.

TOP 10 KARATE MOVES 4–7

As karateka train hard in a *dojo*, they learn more complex moves. These require perfect concentration, form and timing.

4 **Gyaku-zuki (reverse punch)**
Starting in the lunge punch position, the karateka punches with the left arm as she steps forward with the right leg (or the other way round). Performed with a thrust forward of both hips, *gyaku-zuki* is a fast, strong move.

5 **Knife-hand block**
Blocking moves (*uke*) are the main form of defence in karate. For a knife-hand block the karateka uses a cutting action with a flat hand to deflect an attack, such as a straight punch to the head or body.

6 Jodan uke

The *jodan uke* is a high block that uses a raised forearm, rising from the chest to above the head. It is designed to block an attack to the head or upper body.

7 Mawashi geri

Mawashi geri is a powerful roundhouse kick. It starts with the karateka bringing his knee up to his hip with his lower leg folded in. Turning on his supporting foot, he snaps his kicking leg forward at the target. This can often deliver a winning blow in competitions.

KUMITE

Kumite or 'partner work' are forms of sparring training or contests. Some *kumite* in a *dojo* involve two karateka making a series of agreed moves as training. Other forms of *kumite* are more competitive.

Competition kumite

World Karate Federation (WKF) bouts last for three minutes for men and two minutes for women and juniors. Competitions take place on an 8 x 8 metre mat. The action is incredibly intense as both karateka try to score points. Different moves score either one (*ippon*), two (*nihan*) or three (*sanbon*) points.

THE SEVEN SCORING AREAS

Areas that can be kicked or punched:
* Head
* Face
* Neck
* Abdomen
* Chest
* Back
* Side

Two competitors fight it out in a junior International Karate Friendship contest in Chiba, Japan.

Free sparring

Free sparring (*jiyu-kumite*) in competition or the *dojo* puts opponents against each other to test their basic skills and to help teach them awareness, observation and reactions. For juniors and all except the most experienced karateka, padded safety helmets, footwear and gloves are compulsory.

Winning

Officials judge whether a move scores based on many factors, including timing. The karateka with the most points at the end of the bout wins. A bout can be stopped early if a competitor gets eight points ahead – he or she is declared the winner.

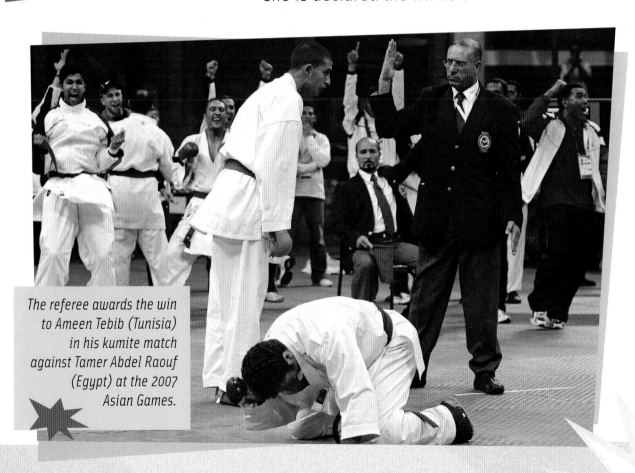

The referee awards the win to Ameen Tebib (Tunisia) in his kumite match against Tamer Abdel Raouf (Egypt) at the 2007 Asian Games.

IN COMPETITION

Karate may not yet be an Olympic sport, but karate competitions are held all over the world. Here are some of the most important events:

European Championships

Held every year since 1966, the Karate European Championships now has 17 different events. The 2007 tournament was held in Bratislava in Slovakia, with Italy, Turkey and Spain topping the medal tables.

Asian Games

Karate has been a popular part of the Asian Games since 1994. There are team and individual events, and six weight divisions for men's *kumite* and four for women's.

The Asian Games are held every four years; the next games will be in 2010 in the Chinese city of Guangzhou.

Japan's Tetsuya Furukawa took gold in the individual kata at the 2006 Asian Games.

World Championships

The World Championships is the ultimate karate competition. It is organised by the World Karate Federation (WKF) and is held every two years. The 2006 WKF World Championships were held in Tampere, Finland.

TOP MEDALLISTS AT 2006 WKF WORLD CHAMPIONSHIPS

Country	Gold	Silver	Bronze
Italy	5	1	1
Japan	2	3	4
Spain	2	2	2
France	2	1	2
Iran	2	0	2

THE FIRST WORLD CHAMPIONS

The first World Championships in Tokyo, Japan, in 1970 contained just two events – an individual competition and a team competition, both for men only. Japan scooped all three team medals although their 'E' team won gold and their 'A' team finished with no medals!

TOP 10 KARATE MOVES 8—10

Surprise is a vital weapon in karate and the back kick and palm heel strike can be unexpected. Sometimes, a combination of moves can also surprise an opponent.

8 **Shotei uchi (palm heel strike)**

Palm heel strikes can be used to attack the stomach or head. With a firm wrist, the arm is thrust towards the target, snapping in then out like the strike of a snake. The padded bottom part of the palm, known as the heel, is the impact area with the fingers and thumb pulled back.

9 Ushiro geri (back kick)

Ushiro geri was designed as a self-defence move when attacked from behind. The karateka turns his back to the direction of the kick, looks over his shoulder and thrusts his kicking foot back with the heel leading.

10 Block and backfist

In sparring competitions, karateka try to make their moves in combinations. Some involve a block to stop an opponent's attack, followed immediately by a strike. One such combination is to block an opponent's punch and then attack with a backfist. The fist is snapped out in a straight line so that the back of the hand connects.

FAMOUS KARATEKA

To be a great kareteka takes dedication, skill, spirit and great ability. Here are three famous karateka from around the world.

The one and only

A 10th-dan black belt is the highest rank possible in karate. Hirokazu Kanazawa (b.1931) from Japan is the only living person in the world to be one! He started with judo but took up karate as a teenager.

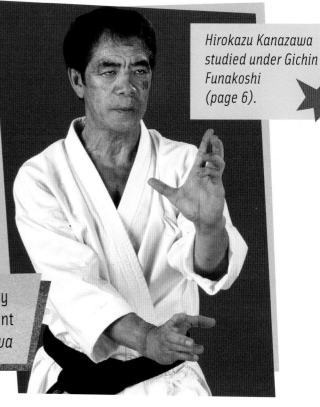

Hirokazu Kanazawa studied under Gichin Funakoshi (page 6).

"The most important points of my teaching are breathing, movement and timing." – *Hirokazu Kanazawa*

Hawaii's history maker

In 2002, Hawaii's Elisa Au became the first American woman to win a World Championship title. She repeated the feat in 2004 in the *kumite* sparring, over 60kg division, and came second at the 2005 World Games – all by the age of 24!

Elisa Au (right) faces up to Yadira Lira of Mexico during the Titan Games held in California, USA.

28

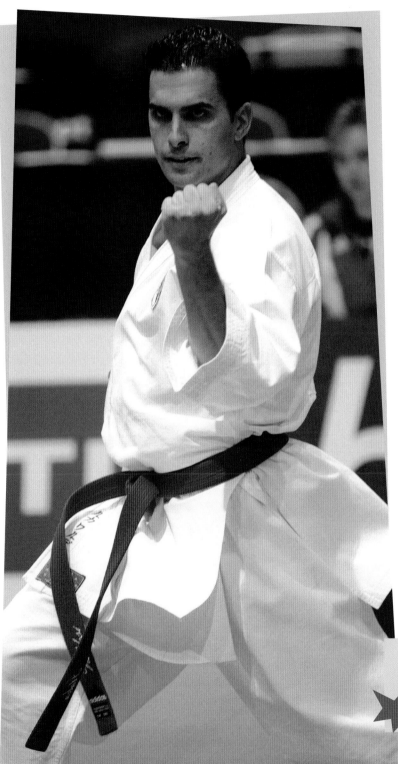

Kata champion

Italy's Luca Valdesi is the undisputed world number one at *kata*. Famous for his fast yet precise movements, he has won a staggering eight European Championships in a row (2000–07), two World Championships and has notched up a total of 77 gold medals!

"Every time that I train, I always attempt to give the maximum…It's my idea of karate." – *Luca Valdesi*

Luca Valdesi performs a move from a kata at the Italian Open Championships in 2006.

GLOSSARY

blocks
Moves used to stop an opponent's punch or kick from striking their intended target area.

bout
A karate contest, usually a *kumite* sparring contest, between two people.

compulsory
Something that you must do.

dachi
Stances.

dan
The rank or level of a person practising karate.

dojo
A training hall for karate and other martial arts.

geri
The Japanese word for kicking in karate.

gi
A special outfit worn when performing karate.

kata
A series of movements.

kiai
The shout you make as you perform a move or strike an opponent.

kumite
Sparring when two people perform.

ju-jitsu
A Japanese martial art.

martial arts
Different fighting sports.

meditating
Relaxing and clearing thoughts from your mind so you can concentrate.

occupied
An area of one country where another country has taken control.

philosophy
A set of beliefs or aims about life, and ways of thinking and acting.

sensei
A karate teacher or instructor.

stances
How you stand, position your feet and balance your weight.

zuki
The Japanese word for punching in karate.

FURTHER INFORMATION

BOOKS

There are lots of instructional books available on karate. Check out your local library for books that suit you. The only way to really learn, though, is by joining a karate school.

Learn Karate

J. Allen Queen (Sterling Publishing, 2000)
A really good guide for beginners to the basic techniques involved in karate, with step by step series of images.

Karate

Sanette Smit (New Holland, 2001)
A colourful photographic guide to karate techniques and philosophy with dozens of colour photographs.

Karate-Do: My Way of Life

Gichin Funakoshi (1997)
A short but amazing book about the life of the founder of Shokotan Karate, it's packed with little nuggets of wisdom and sayings.

DVDs AND MOVIES

Some of these movies are not suitable for all ages:

Simply Karate (Mark Richardson, Hinkler Books / Penton Overseas Inc, 2004)
This package contains a 64-page book and a DVD of basic karate moves, tips and techniques. Just perfect to get your mind ready for a trip to a karate club.

The Karate Kid (John G. Avildsen, 1984)
Sure, it's old and a bit cheesy, but any kid into karate has to see *The Karate Kid*, just the once. Watch out for the sequels, *KK II*

and *III* and the 1994 movie, *The Next Karate Kid* which starred Hilary Swank as a young karateka.

Shotokan Karate - A Beginner's Guide

(Hosted by *Sensei* Jonathan Bolt, 2007)
Features moves performed in slow-motion to help beginners – and even comes with traditional Japanese background music!

WEBSITES

http://www.kugb.org
Homepage of the Karate Union of Great Britain, this website lists lots of karate clubs around the UK. Hopefully, there will be one or more near you.

http://www.theshotokanway.com
This excellent website is absolutely packed with articles, interviews and features, including a large beginners section and a calendar of events. Set aside plenty of hours to surf these webpages.

http://www.karateworld.org
This is the website for the World Karate Federation, the biggest organisation involved in karate.

http://www.shotokankarate.org.uk
This handy website has a great karate book list as well as bite-sized pages on *kumite* sparring and some great *kata* videos.

INDEX

These are the lists of contents for the titles in Combat Sports:

Boxing
What is boxing? • Round 1 - the birth of modern boxing • A controversial sport • Boxing's top moves: punches • Getting into boxing • On the road • Boxing's top moves: defence • Making weight • Boxing at the movies • Competition • Boxing at the Olympics • Great champions • Ali: The greatest • Glossary • Further information • Index

Judo
Introducing judo • The origins of judo • The gentle way • Top 10 judo moves - 1-4 • The spread of judo • Respect and discipline • Top 10 judo moves - 5-7 • Modern judo • Clubs and dojos • Judo competition • Olympic judo • Top 10 judo moves - 8-10 • Famous judoka • Glossary • Further information • Index

Karate
What is karate? • Karate's origins • Karate spreads around the world • Karate at the movies • At the dojo • Karate today • Top 10 karate moves - 1-3 • Mind and body • Top 10 karate moves - 4-7 • Kumite • In competition • Top 10 karate moves - 8-10 • Famous karateka • Glossary • Further information • Index

Kickboxing
What is kickboxing? • Kickboxing origins • Muay Thai • Modern kickboxing • All the rage • In training • Top 10 kickboxing moves - 1-3 • Strong mind, strong body • Sparring • Top 10 kickboxing moves - 4-7 • Competition kickboxing • Top 10 kickboxing moves -8-10 • Famous kickboxers • Glossary • Further information • Index

Taekwondo
What is taekwondo? • Ancient martial arts • Spreading around the world • Top 10 taekwondo moves - 1-4 • The discipline of taekwondo • Fit mind, fit body • Top 10 taekwondo moves - 5-7 • Modern taekwondo • Clubs and dojang • Taekwondo competition • Taekwondo at the Olympics • Top 10 taekwondo moves - 8-10 • Famous fighters • Glossary • Further information • Index

Wrestling
What is wrestling? • An ancient history • Wrestling around the world • Folk wrestling • Wrestling today • In training • Top 10 wrestling moves - 1-3 • Mind and body • Professional wrestling • Top 10 wrestling moves - 4-6 • Wrestling at the Olympics • Top 10 wrestling moves - 7-10 • Famous wrestlers • Glossary • Further information • Index